Tea
A Recipe and Guidebook

Quick and Easy to Make

Tea Recipes That Are

Nutritious, Relaxing, and Energizing.

Includes Recipes for: Black, Green, White, Oolong, and Herbal Teas

Disclaimer

All rights Reserved. No part of this publication or the information in it may be quoted from or reproduced in any form by means such as printing, scanning, photocopying or otherwise without prior written permission of the copyright holder.

Disclaimer and Terms of Use: Effort has been made to ensure that the information in this book is accurate and complete, however, the author and the publisher do not warrant the accuracy of the information, text and graphics contained within the book due to the rapidly changing nature of science, research, known and unknown facts and internet. The author and the publisher do not hold any responsibility for errors, omissions or contrary interpretation of the subject matter herein. This book is presented solely for motivational and informational purposes only.

Introduction

After water, tea is the most popular beverage in the world. Recent statistics suggest that, on a daily basis, 165 million cups of tea are consumed around the globe. Human beings have enjoyed the taste and health benefits of tea for centuries.

There's something special and magical about tea that makes it an enduring beverage-of-choice among millions around the planet. Tea is an extraordinary drink and a symbol of nature's endless bounty that hasn't just crossed physical, political, and cultural boundaries, but has also become a symbol of quiet pleasures, relaxation, and joy. Tea isn't a rich people drink, or a poor people drink; it's above all the artificial differences. Tea is everyone's drink. Although tea has received its fair share of bad press – *remember the American Revolution kicked off by the Boston Tea Party?* – tea is a timeless beverage with a delicious taste and the most amazing, undeniable health benefits a drink can offer. In fact, tea is a drink of love that brings people together all around the globe.

When I think about my childhood I remember that tea was a constant presence through both the happiest and the darkest of days experienced by our family. It always brought us together and allowed us to celebrate the good times and gain peace of mind and relaxation in times of difficulty. We drank a variety of teas in the morning, with lunch, and in the evening. When we didn't have anything to do, we drank tea. When we were stressed because so much was going on, we drank tea still. I used to sniff the tin that my mother kept her tea in because I loved the aroma; I still do (I have an embarrassing habit of sniffing my teabags). I distinctly remember the fragrance that spread throughout the house when tea was being prepared; it was sweet, beautiful and has become a permanently vivid childhood memory.

My mother took special pride in preparing tea for everyone. She loved it and her love was felt in every sip – honest, pure, and perfect. It is in honor of that most precious kind of love that I present to you a collection of some of the most delicious tasting tea recipes from around the world!

Enjoy!

With Love,

Jenna Mars

Table of Contents

Brief History of Tea

Tea has travelled throughout the world, spreading to virtually every country on the planet. It has a long history, which spans across centuries. Even though it is often thought of as a British drink, the history of tea goes way beyond days of the British Empire.

The history of tea is rather fascinating and gives interesting insight into the history of world. It is believed that tea originated in China as a medicinal drink as far back as 2737 BCE. For several centuries, people drank tea because of its herbal and medicinal qualities. It seems that tea became an everyday drink around 300 CE and became known for assisting in the digestion process, which is why the Chinese used to drink it after their meals.

Tea was initially introduced to Japanese monks who had travelled to China for spiritual studies. It then became a vital part of Japanese culture as well. They developed the "Japanese Tea Ceremony" where they served the tea in a sacred, spiritual ceremony.

During the seventeenth century, drinking tea became popular in Europe, especially Great Britain. The British East India Company started the tea trade between China and Britain. To overcome the Chinese monopoly within the trade, the British began tea production in India. They established tea plantations across India in order to reduce their dependency on Chinese tea. Tea was initially referred to as a Chinese drink and was regarded as a medicine, rather than a fashionable beverage that it later became.

The Dutch initially brought tea to America in the seventeenth century. The English, who later acquired the Dutch colony, passed on their tea drinking custom to America. Tea has gained significant popularity throughout American history and is still thriving today.

Tea Plant

Tea is made from cured leaves of *Camellia sinensis* plant. *Camellia sinensis* is described as a healing herb that promotes good health and longevity. It has a slightly bitter and astringent flavor. It contains an amino acid - *L-theanine* - that helps the mind stay alert and focused.

Tea has a multitude of other health benefits making it a great choice of a supplement to any diet. There are numerous varieties of tea that are available based on the region it is cultivated in, the time of the year when picked, and the processing method used. However, on a broader level tea can be categorized into four major types: Green tea, Black tea, White tea, and Oolong tea. Each of these four types is made from the same plant. The variety and processing of the plant after it is harvested determines the type of tea it becomes. We will explore each type of tea and how it is processed, followed by some delicious recipes for each kind.

Health Benefits of Tea

Anti-aging: Antioxidants present in tea help to protect the body against the aging process. White tea extract helps fight against the formation of wrinkles. Tea may also provide protection against ultraviolet rays.

Detoxification: Tea can be used as a natural cleanser. Detoxify the body of built up toxins by following a tea diet for 1-7 days. A detox involves drinking a specific tea in the morning to supply the body with antioxidants, vitamins, nutrients and electrolytes for the day. Then throughout the day, Green tea may be consumed. Finally at night, drinking a tea that contains natural laxative effects can help to cleanse the colon.

Less Caffeine: Tea contains less caffeine than coffee. Coffee usually contains two or three times the caffeine as compared to tea.

Healthier Heart: Tea helps in keeping the arteries unclogged and reduces the risk of stroke and heart attack. A study in the Netherlands found that the people who drank two to three cups of black tea per day, had a 70% reduced risk of heart ailments compared to non-tea drinkers.

Strong Bones: Tea helps in maintaining stronger bones, courtesy of the phytochemicals present in it. Green tea in particular helps improve bone density and strength.

Improved Dental Health: Fluoride and tannins contained in tea offer protection against plaque formation on teeth. Plaque build-up leads to bad breath, among other dental problems. Studies have shown that tea can provide up to 70% of the fluorides needed by the body.

Protection against Cancer: Polyphenols, one of the anti-oxidants found in tea, help to fight against cancer.

Protection against Diabetes: Caffeine content in tea helps to reduce the overall risk of diabetes, including type 2 diabetes.

Zero calories: Tea alone doesn't contain any calories unless you add sweetener, milk, or other ingredients to it.

Improved metabolism: Tea is good news for people who have a slow metabolic rate and are struggling to lose weight. Green tea helps in burning 70-80 additional calories per day given that about four cups are consumed per day. Green tea extracts interfere with fat formation in the body. In turn, this results in improved muscle endurance.

Improved vision: Green tea components help with better functioning of eye tissues, especially retina tissues.

Stress Buster: Stressed out? Black tea is the best choice to help relax you. According to research, black tea may help reduce stress hormone levels in the blood. It also helps to lower high blood pressure associated with stress.

A Guide to Brewing the Best Tea

Here are some important guidelines to follow in order to brew the best cup of tea, one that is well-steeped and balanced.

Is there such a thing as the "right water" for your tea?

There is, but it's really hard to get unless you have a gushing glacial spring in your backyard. Water varies in contaminants, minerals, and oxygen levels, which changes the quality of brewed tea. The best type of water you can use for tea has little mineral content, a neutral pH level, and minimal quantity of dissolved compounds. Experts recommend water from a glacial spring that is filtered, not too soft, has no smell and has no taste. Tap water is not the best choice because it typically has contaminants added to purify the water including chlorine and fluoride. Distilled water is also not good to use because it gives a flat taste. Although this might make it seem like getting the "right water" is impossible, we recommend spring water (bottled is oaky, but we know the quality of bottled water varies) or water that has undergone filtering. Tap water quality can of course be increased through boiling and filtering.

Preheat the pot!

Pre heat the pot or cup you are going to brew the tea in by filling it with hot water and letting it sit. Discard the water used to heat the pot or cup. Next, add fresh water into the preheated pot and steep the tea.

How much tea is good tea?

That depends on your preference and the tea's strength. However, the quantity of tea which is recommended in a serving depends on the type and strength of the tea. One teaspoon of tea to every one cup of water is a general guideline for good taste and strength. For a stronger tea, you can add more of the tea and steep it for a longer period of time.

What's the perfect temperature?

Black tea: The best black tea is prepared with water which is close to boiling. It should then be removed from the heat, settled for a minute and then tea should be added. The temperature should be between 190°F and 200°F.

Green tea: Temperature should be less than boiling point i.e. 170°F to 180°F.

White tea: Boiled water, which is then cooled to 160°F to 180°F.

Oolong tea: Don't fully boil water. Before it starts to boil, remove from the heat and add the tea. Temperatures should be around 170°F to 180°F.

Herbal tea: The best temperature for herbal tea is 160°F.

How much time to set for steeping?

It's up to you! The steeping time will change the strength of the tea, of course. If you want a stronger tea, then steep for more time. If you wish for mild tea, steep for only a minute or two. Some teas, like black or herbal, need more time (more than 5 minutes) to extract all the flavor and the amazing nutrients.

Onto the recipes, we go!

Black Tea Recipes

Black tea, like all other major teas, is made from the *Camellia sinensis* shrub. With black tea, the leaves are allowed to wither, and then they are rolled. They sit and ferment until they become black, at which point the leaves are heated to 200 degrees Fahrenheit. This stops the fermenting process. The tea is then dried and crushed. Black tea is the most common type of tea; it is bitter in taste and contains more caffeine compared to other tea preparations. Typically, one bag of tea that is steeped for five minutes contains approximately 47 mg. of caffeine. It also contains antioxidant components known as *theaflavins* and *thearubigins*, which help to decrease cholesterol level and risk of stroke.

Enjoy this collection of black tea drinks, some dating back centuries!

Chai Tea (Masala Tea)

"Chai" is a Hindi word for tea. This tea is prepared with black tea leaves, Indian spices, and milk. Using sugar is optional but enjoyed by many, of course taking away from the health benefits a little. But, sweet Indian chai is delicious to taste, and can be healthy too in some aspects. Chai tea offers a blend of health benefits coming from both the tea and the spices. Benefits include antioxidants, anti-viral and anti-cancer properties. In addition:

- *Cardamom: improves circulation, reduces respiratory allergies, detoxifies the body, and improves digestion*
- *Cloves: have anti-bacterial properties*
- *Cinnamon: has anti-inflammatory components*
- *Ginger: boosts immune system*

Serving size: makes 4 cups
Brewing time: 25 minutes

Ingredients:

3 cup water

1 cup low fat milk

2 black tea bags (single serve)

6 pods green cardamom

6 cloves

1 cinnamon stick

1 inch ginger, peeled and finely chopped

4 black peppercorns

2 tbsp. brown sugar

Directions:

1. Take a pot and combine all the spices together with water. Bring the combination to a boil over high heat, then reduce the heat to low and simmer for 5 minutes, covered.

2. Again boil the pot and add the tea. Remove from the heat and steep for 3 minutes.

3. Pass the tea through a mesh sieve to strain the solids out. Be careful to catch it all!

4. Then transfer the tea back to the pot and add sugar and milk. Stir well and heat for 1-2 minutes.

5. Serve by pouring the tea into cups. You can garnish with a cinnamon stick.

Nutrition facts per serving:
Calories: 60
Carbs: 12 g
Fat: 0 g
Protein: 2 g
Sodium: 32 mg
Sugar: 6 g

Black Tea with Milk

This tea is best as a morning drink served with crackers, cookies/biscuits, or other bread as the caffeine content will help give you a morning boost. The tea is rich in calcium, phosphorus, riboflavin and vitamins, while having a good taste. The milk and sugar help smooth the bitter taste of the tea.

Serving size: make 1 serving
Brewing time: 10 minutes

Ingredients:

1 tsp loose black tea

¾ cup of water

¼ cup of low-fat milk

1 tsp sugar

Directions:

1. Boil water in a pot.
2. Add the tea and sugar.
3. Cover and simmer for 5 minutes on low heat.
4. Steep for 3 minutes.
5. Add milk, stir and again heat for a minute.
6. Strain through a mesh sieve and serve in a small cup.

Nutrition facts per serving:
Calories: 42

Carbs: 7.3g
Protein .4g
Vitamins: A and B12
Calcium: 8%
Sodium: 32mg
Sugar: 7.4g
Cholesterol: 3mg

Black Tea with Lemon Balm

People who like lemon flavor would really enjoy this healthy tea infused with lemon balm. Lemon balm comes from the mint family or perennial herbs. It has been used for medicinal purposes to relieve digestive problems, pain, mental disorders and in aromatherapy. It is known to have a calming effect. If you are stressed, having headaches, toothaches or having stomach problems, this tea may help relieve your symptoms.

Serving size: makes 1 serving
Brewing time: 10 minutes

Ingredients:

1 c. water

1 bag black tea

1 tsp. dried lemon balm

Lemon peel

Directions:

1. Boil water in a pot.

2. Add all ingredients listed above and remove from the heat, cover and steep the tea for 5 minutes or more.

3. Warm a serving cup with hot water. Discard water.

4. Strain and serve hot tea in the heated cup.

Nutrition facts per serving:
Calories: 5
Sodium: 1mg

Dark Chocolate Chai Latte

In this recipe we are using a blend of Indian spices and cacao. This chai tea is a treat that can be shared among friends as a dessert or sweet breakfast boost. It can be served warm in the winter or over ice in the summer. This drink contains the benefits of chai listed above, along with those of raw cacao. Cacao is a rich source of antioxidants and it also gives the brain a boost of positive mood. You will fall in love with this tasty black tea.

Serving size: make 7 servings
Brewing time: 15 minutes

Ingredients:

2 c. water

4 bags black tea

4 c. milk

½ c. raw cacao powder

1/2 c. brown sugar or honey

6 cardamom pods

1 piece ginger (1 inch)

1 tsp. mixture of whole cloves, ground cinnamon and black peppercorns

Directions:

1. In a large saucepan, bring water to a boil.

2. Add in all of the ingredients except for the tea. Stir over medium heat for 2 minutes.

3. Add the tea bags, cover the saucepan and simmer for 10 minutes over low heat.

4. Mix well and then strain through a mesh sieve into a pitcher.

5. Discard solids.

6. Serve hot in cups.

Nutrition facts per serving:
Calories: 350
Carbs: 34 g
Cholesterol: 60 mg
Sodium: 105 mg
Potassium: 110mg
Protein: 7g
Vitamins: A (10%), C (4%), calcium (25%), iron (10%)

Indian Cardamom Tea (*Elaichi* Tea)

This tea is an Indian style tea. It combines the flavor of cardamom with the bitter black tea. Drinking the tea makes you feel warm and refreshed. This tea can be taken any time of the day with crackers, cookies/biscuits, or toast. The seeds of cardamom are used to help with digestive problems and the common cold. If you are feeling under the weather or have indigestion, a cup full of this cardamom tea can help get things moving.

Serving size: make 4-6 servings
Brewing time: 10 minutes

Ingredients:

5 c. water

4 bags black tea

5-6 green cardamom pods

2 black cardamom

1 c. hot milk

4 tbsp. sugar

Directions:

1. Crush both types of cardamom in a mortar and pestle.

2. Bring water to boil in a medium saucepan.

3. Lower the heat and add the tea bags, sugar and cardamom. Simmer for 5 minutes more.

4. Remove the pan from the heat and pour in the milk, strain and serve hot

Nutrition facts per serving:
Calories: 75
Carbs: 16 g
Fat: 0 g
Protein 2 g
Sodium: 32 mg
Sugar: 12 g

Mulled Black Tea

This recipe is very easy and delicious. It is a spicy variation of tea containing black tea leaves, cinnamon, cloves, berries, and orange-lemon rind. This is a great tea to drink when feeling low-energy or experiencing digestive problems.

- *Allspice berries come from a plant and have been known to help with digestion, the common cold, diabetes and high blood pressure.*
- *Cinnamon is used as an appetite stimulant, digestion assistant and soother for menstrual cramps, the flu and colds.*
- *Cloves: are helpful to aid in digestion.*

Serving size: make 2 servings
Brewing time: 7-8 minutes

Ingredients:

2 c. water

4 tsp. loose black tea

2 tsp. coarsely crushed cinnamon stick

4 cloves

6 whole allspice berries

1 tsp. each grated orange rind and lemon rind

Directions:

1. Boil water in a medium saucepan.

2. Put all of the ingredients in a tea ball and place it into the boiling water.

3. Simmer for 5 minutes over low heat.

4. Remove the tea ball and pour the tea into a warm cup.

5. Enjoy!

Nutrition facts per serving:
Calories: 12
Carbs: 4 g
Sodium: .5 mg

Cinnamon & Black Pepper Tea

In this tea we are using ingredients that are helpful in soothing a sore throat. The combination of pepper, lemon, and cinnamon helps to fight cold and flu symptoms. Lemon is a great source of magnesium, Vitamin C, calcium and bioflavonoids. These are helpful in nursing the body back to health.

Serving size: makes 1 serving
Brewing time: 5 minutes

Ingredients

1 bag black tea
1 c. water
1 stick (1 inch) cinnamon
1 tsp. lemon juice
¼ tsp. black pepper

Directions

1. Boil the water in a small saucepan.
2. Add cinnamon, black pepper, the tea bag and lemon juice.
3. Remove the pan from the heat. Cover and steep for 5 minutes.
4. Strain into a cup.
5. Enjoy warm.

Nutrition facts per serving:
Calories: 22
Carbs: 6 g
Sodium: 3 mg

Green Tea Recipes

Green tea has its origins in China but is now widely consumed all over the world. The process of making tea into green tea involves minimal oxidation of the leaves. Green tea is prepared by quick-drying of the unfermented tealeaves of the Camellia sinensis shrub. This tea is complimented by different flavors such as lemon and mint. It retains more health benefits than other teas because of the minimal oxidation. The average amount of caffeine from 1 bag of green tea that is brewed for 5 minutes is approximately 20 mg.

Chinese Green Mint Tea

This tea is best to drink after a meal as it helps with digestion. The tea features fresh mint leaves, which bring a multitude of benefits for the body. For an increased influence of mint, increase the steep time. Sugar or honey can be added to taste.

- *Mint: Mint leaves have been known to clear up congestion in the lungs, throat and nose. Mint can also assist in weight-loss, reduce allergies, relieve depression, promote digestion, reduce nausea, relieve acne, and improve oral health.*

Serving size: makes 6 servings
Brewing time: 8 minutes

Ingredients:

6 c. water

½ c. fresh mint leaves

1 tbsp. Chinese green tea

1/4 c. sugar

Directions:

1. Boil the water in a pot.

2. Take a teapot, rinse it with hot water and place the green tea and mint leaves in it.

3. Pour hot water into the teapot over the leave mixture.

4. Steep the tea for 5 minutes.

5. Stir and strain into cups.

6. Add sugar to your taste liking, stir well and serve hot.

Nutrition facts per serving:
Calories: 45
Carbs: 11 g
Fat: .16 g
Protein .8 g
Sodium: 6 mg
Sugar: 8 g

Rosemary Energy Green Tea

Rosemary leaves are known to help fight against illnesses, being a great source of calcium, vitamin B6 and iron. Rosemary brings a unique and enjoyable flavor to the green tea in this recipe. The two combined offer an energy boosting effect.

- *Rosemary is an herb that has historically been used to help the immune system, improve memory, relieve muscle pain, and stimulate hair growth.*

Serving size: makes 1 serving
Brewing time: 8 minutes

Ingredients:

1 c. water

½ tsp. loose green tea

1 tsp. rosemary

1 tsp. honey (optional)

Pinch of nutmeg powder

Directions:

1. Place the rosemary and green tea in a teapot.
2. Pour hot water over them.
3. Steep for 7 minutes or more.
4. Add honey if desired and stir.
5. Strain into a cup and enjoy hot.

Nutrition facts per serving:
Calories: 67
Carbs: 16 g
Sodium: 1 mg
Sugar: 16 g

Honeydew Mint Iced Tea

This tea gives you a unique taste of melon and mint in a tea. It is refreshing over ice in the afternoon or warm in the morning. The honeydew offers benefits of iron, B vitamins and other essential nutrients.

Serving size: make 8 servings
Brewing time: 15-20 minutes

Ingredients

8 c. water

3 c. honeydew melon, peeled and cubed

5 bags green tea

1/3 c. sugar

1 c. mint leaves

Directions:

1. Add 8 cups boiling water into a teapot, add the teabags into it. Steep for 5 minutes.

2. Boil melon, sugar, and mint leaves in a saucepan with some water. Reduce heat and simmer for 8-10 minutes.

3. Remove teabags from tea and pour it over the melon mixture.

4. Cool for 30 minutes and then refrigerate for about 2 hrs.

5. Take out from refrigerator and strain well so as solid part remains separate.

6. Serve clear beverage with ice cubes.

Nutrition facts per serving:
Calories: 58
Carbs: 14g
Fat: .12g
Protein .4g
Sodium: 12 mg
Sugar: 13 g
Vitamins: C (18%)

Citrus Iced Tea

This homemade citrus tea is refreshing and offers a light dose of nutrients. Citrus fruits have long been used for medicinal purposes because of their high potency of vitamin C, niacin, thiamin, vitamin B6, phosphorus, magnesium, copper riboflavin and more. This tea is great if you feel a cold coming on.

Serving size: make 6 servings
Brewing time: 12 minutes

Ingredients:

6 c. water

6 bags green tea

3 slices of each lemon, sweet lime and oranges

¼ c. sugar

Directions:

1. In a teapot add the lemon, lime, orange and tea bags.

2. Pour boiling water over them and steep for 10 minutes.

3. Stir well and strain into a large container.

4. Add sugar and stir again to dissolve. Let it cool down.

5. Pour over ice in the glasses to serve iced tea.

Nutrition facts per serving:
Calories: 34

Carbs: 33.5 g
Fat: 0 g
Protein .1 g
Sodium: 0 mg
Sugar 33 g.
Iron: 1%

Avocado Iced Green Tea Smoothie Recipe

This is a unique combination of ingredients that blend spicy, creamy, and sour together. The resulting tea smoothie is packed with antioxidants, healthy fats, caffeine, vitamins and minerals. This can be used as a meal replacement, recommended for lunch or dinner.

Serving size: make 2 servings
Brewing time: 15 minutes

Ingredients

1 c. water

2 bags green tea

2 tbsp. grapefruit juice

¼ tsp. diced Serrano chili pepper

½ avocado

½ tsp. ginger paste

1 tsp. lemon juice

Directions:

1. Steep the tea with water for 5 minutes.

2. In a blender, blend the remaining ingredients to make a smooth paste/puree.

3. Strain the tea and pour it into the fruit mixture. Turn the blender to mix well with the tea.

4. Serve immediately in iced glasses.

Nutrition facts per serving:
Calories: 133
Carbs: 5 g
Fat: 5.5 g
Protein: .5 g
Sodium: 14 mg
Sugar .5 g

White Tea Recipes

White tea is trimmed from both the buds and leaves of the Camellia sinensis. The plucked leaves are placed in natural sunlight to whither and minimally oxidize then are processed to stop the oxidation process. This tea has the highest amount of antioxidants compared to green and black teas. The tea is known to reduce blood pressure and cholesterol while improving circulation. On average, 1 bag of white tea that is brewed for 5 minutes contains approximately 15 mg. of caffeine.

An interesting benefit to animals is that white tea protects them from pathogenic bacteria such as Salmonella!

Original White Tea

Enjoy the pure taste and essence of white tea. By making it a habit to drink a cup of white tea each day, you will reap the health benefits of antioxidants, cancer prevention, low blood pressure, bone strength, heart protection and lowered cholesterol.

Serving size: makes 1 serving
Brewing time: 10 minutes

Ingredients:

1 c. pure water

2 tsp. loose white tea leaves

Directions:

1. Warm your teacup with hot water.
2. Add tealeaves into the cup.
3. Boil water and pour onto the tealeaves.
4. Cover and steep for 5 minutes.
5. Open, stir once and again steep for 2 minutes.
6. Re steep to extract additional nutrients from the tea.
7. Strain tea in serving cup and serve.

Nutrition facts per serving:
Calories: 0
Carbs: 0 g
Sodium: 0 mg

Peach White Iced Tea

Sweet peach tea is great over ice in the summer time. Peaches bring a great flavor along with health benefits for nerve and cell health, antioxidants, immune system health, and blood circulation.

Serving size: make 8 servings
Brewing time: 20 minutes

Ingredients:

8 c. water

5 bags white tea

1/3 c. sugar

4 c. peaches, peeled and sliced

Directions

1. Combine the tea into a pot of boiling water. Reduce the heat and steep the tea for 5 minutes.

2. In a large saucepan, boil the peaches and sugar in 1 cup of water.

3. Simmer the mixture until the peaches become soft. (10-12 minutes).

4. Discard tea bags and pour the tea into a saucepan over the peaches.

5. Mix well and refrigerate the mixture for 2 hours.

6. Strain out the clear beverage in a pitcher.

7. Serve in 8 tall glasses with ice cubes with fresh slices of peaches to garnish.

Nutrition facts per serving:
Calories: 65
Carbs: 16g
Protein: 1g
Sodium: 15 mg
Vitamins: A and C

White Tea Sangria

This tea is rich in fruits and a source of fiber to help with digestion. Use different fruits that are easily available on hand preferably those in season are best to use. This sangria includes alcohol, so make sure children aren't enticed by the colorful fruits inside.

Serving size: make 8-10 servings
Brewing time: 5 minutes

Ingredients:

4 c. water

1 bottle white wine

4 tbsp. loose white tea

6-10 each berries and grapes

2 c. white grape juice

All fruits should be washed and sliced (1 orange, 2 kiwis, 1 lime, 1 peach, 1 apple and 1 lemon)

Directions:

1. Steep the tea with hot water in a teapot for 5 minutes.
2. Strain the tea into a pitcher. Let it cool, then transfer it into the refrigerator.
3. Mix all the fruits with the chilled tea and wine.
4. Serve over ice in tall glasses and enjoy.

Nutrition facts per serving:
Calories: 101
Carbs: 7 g
Fat: .10g
Protein .2 g
Sodium: 1 mg
Sugar: 1 g

White Orange Iced Tea

This citrus tea is rich in antioxidants and loaded with vitamin C, offering benefits for boosting the immune system.

Serving size: make 2 servings
Brewing time: 12 minutes

Ingredients:

1 c. water

½ c. fresh squeezed orange juice

2 bags white tea

Directions:

1. Boil a pot of water, then remove it from the heat.

2. Steep the tea for 5 minutes.

3. Let it cool and then add the orange juice.

4. Stir well and serve immediately in 2 tall glasses over ice.

5. Enjoy chilled.

Nutrition facts per serving:
Calories: 28
Carbs: 6.5 g
Fat: 0g
Protein .5 g
Sodium: .5 mg
Sugar: 5 g

Blueberry White Tea

In this remedy-tea we are using natural sweetness from dried blueberries and vanilla. Vanilla, mint, blueberries and hibiscus give a well-rounded flavor to the tea.

Serving size: make 4 servings
Brewing time: 10-12 minutes

Ingredients:

4 c. water

2 tsp. loose white tea

1 vanilla bean, chopped

¼ tsp. dried peppermint

3 tsp. dried blueberries

2 strips of orange peel (about 5 inch)

½ c. dried hibiscus

Directions

1. Bring water to a boil in a pot.
2. Add all the ingredients given above to the tea.
3. Boil the mixture and steep for 5 minutes. Steep longer for more extraction.
4. Stir and then simmer the tea for 3 minutes.
5. Strain the tea with a fine mesh or coffee filter.

6. Serve hot immediately.

Nutrition facts per serving:
Calories: 8.5
Carbs: 2 g
Fat: 0 g
Protein 0 g
Sodium: .5 mg
Sugar: 1.2 g.

Oolong Tea Recipes

The word "oolong" is a Chinese word meaning "black dragon." Oolong tea is produced by a unique process of drying under the tealeaves under strong sun, oxidation, and then curling the leaves. This tea is similar to black tea, but is fermented for less time. On average, 1 bag of oolong tea that is brewed for 5 minutes contains about 30 mg. of caffeine. This may help to lower the triglyceride levels, as well as offer assistance with weight loss.

Thai Iced Tea

In Thailand, this tea is called "Cha Yen," which means chilled tea. The color of this tea becomes muddy red and it has a strong flavor. A low quality black tea is used to make Cha Yen.

Serving size: make 6 servings
Brewing time: 7-8 minutes

Ingredients:

6 c. water

1 c. oolong tea

1 can evaporated milk

1 c. sugar

Directions:

1. Boil the water in a teapot. Add the tea and remove the pot from the heat.

2. Steep the tea for 5 minutes.

3. Strain in to a pitcher through a mesh.

4. Add the sugar and stir well to dissolve.

5. Cool and refrigerate until the tea is cooled.

6. Serve tea in tall glasses over crushed ice.

7. Stir in 2 tbsp. evaporated milk.

8. Enjoy this sweet and creamy Thai Tea.

Nutrition facts per serving:
Calories: 38
Carbs: 38 g
Fat: 4.6 g
Protein 4g
Sodium: 65 mg
Sugar: 38 g

Sake and Pear Oolong Tea

This tea has a refreshing fruit flavor. It features the soft flavor of pear, sake and oolong tea. Do not boil after adding the sake. This is a great adult beverage to enjoy with friends after dinner. It is great company for Asian dishes such as sushi or teriyaki chicken.

Serving size: make 2 servings
Brewing time: 15 minutes

Ingredients:

3 tsp. oolong tea

¼ c. unfiltered nigori sake

1 c. pear juice

Directions:

1. In a saucepan, combine pear juice and tea. Bring to boil over low heat.

2. Remove from the heat and steep for 4 minutes.

3. Add the sake and simmer the tea again (DO NOT BOIL) for 2 minutes over low heat.

4. Strain in a pot and serve hot.

Nutrition facts per serving:
Calories: 40
Carbs: 5 g
Sodium: 1 mg
Sugar: 3.5 g

White Radish Oolong Tea

Use only white radishes to make this tea. The radishes in this tea are helpful for soothing a cough and sore throat by reducing the mucus in the body. They also help to fight off viral infections, with digestion, to remove toxins and to protect against cancer. The tea gains a strong flavor from the white radish, so it should be used sparingly and balanced with salt.

Serving size: Make 3 servings
Brewing time: 5-7 minutes

Ingredients:

3 c. water

2 tsp. oolong tea

1 inch white radish

Pinch of salt

Directions:

1. Boil water in a teapot.
2. Peel and chop the radish into small pieces.
3. Place the tea, radish and salt into a saucepan.
4. Pour boiled water over them and steep for 3 minutes.
5. Strain and serve the tea slightly hot tea.

Nutrition facts per serving:
Calories: 2.5
Carbs: 1 g
Fat: 0 g
Protein 1 g
Sodium: 50 mg
Sugar: 0 g

Creamy Oolong Chai Iced Tea

This tea is a sweet, creamy and flavorful recipe that can assist with one's weight loss efforts. It is recommended for the morning, before breakfast. This recipe can be helpful for diabetics, as it contains cinnamon, which helps to keep the blood sugar level stable. Cayenne helps by increasing the metabolism. Oolong tea also helps to control weight and the coconut milk helps give a satiated feeling.

Serving size: make 4 servings
Brewing time: 5-7 minutes

Ingredients:

3 c. water

4 tea bags oolong tea

½ c. canned coconut milk

1 tsp. cinnamon powder

2 tsp. honey

1 tsp. vanilla

Pinch of Cayenne

Directions:

1. Boil water and steep tea for 5 minutes.

2. In a blender, take all remaining ingredients and blend to make smooth mixture.

3. Discard tea bags and pour tea in to blender and mix with other ingredients.

4. Serve in 4 glasses having crushed ice.

Nutrition facts per serving:
Calories: 96
Carbs: 6 g
Fat: 8 g
Protein 2 g
Sodium: 8 mg
Sugar: 6 g

Licorice Tea

Many think of candy when they hear licorice. Licorice root however is an ancient remedy used to help counteract stress and anxiety. The licorice root is said to increase the body's production of the chemical that reduces inflammation and promotes healing from the body's stress response system.

Serving size: make 3 servings
Brewing time: 7 minutes

Ingredients

3 c. water

3 tsp. Ginseng Oolong tea

6 pieces of dried licorice root

Directions:

1. Boil water in a pot.

2. Place licorice and tea in to a teapot.

3. Pour the hot water into the pot and steep for 5 minutes.

4. Serve the tea warm.

Nutrition facts per serving:
Calories: 0
Carbs: 0 g
Fat: 0 g
Protein 0 g
Sodium: 0 mg
Sugar: 0 g

Herbal Tea Recipes

Herbal teas differ widely with one another and the general teas because they do not come from the same plant. They are the combinations of flowers, herbs, and dried fruits, which are brewed like tea. Herbal teas contain no caffeine, often lower blood pressure, have delicious flavors, and improve digestion. They also often contain no calories and no sugar.

Raspberry Tea

Raspberries contain a high quantity of tannin; therefore, they are effective for eliminating bad taste. They are also helpful for relief from cramping and nausea. This recipe is also helpful for women who experience pain from their menstrual cycle including, cramping and abdominal pain. This tea is versatile, as it is gentle enough for children, but very useful for adults. Raspberry Tea is a common home remedy for diarrhea as well.

Serving size: make 1 serving
Brewing time: 10 minutes

Ingredients:

1 c. water

¼ c. dried raspberry leaves

¼ c. dried lemon grass

½ c. dried chamomile flowers

½ c. dried orange peel

Directions:

1. Mix all the dried herbs listed above.
2. Boil water.
3. Add 1 tsp. of tea mixture in a cup.
4. Pour hot water over it. Cover and steep for 5-10 minutes. The longer the time, the more tannin is extracted.
5. Consume hot, cold, or iced.

Nutrition facts per serving:
Calories: 40
Carbs: 12 g
Fat: 0 g
Protein 0 g
Sodium: 2 mg
Sugar: 0 g

Hibiscus- Ginger Tea

Hibiscus- ginger tea is a powerhouse of antioxidant components, which help power your body to take control over free radicals that may lead to cancer. This remedy also improves your cardiovascular and skin health.

Serving size: make 4 cups
Brewing time: 15 minutes

Ingredients:

4 c. water

1 tbsp. hibiscus leaves

1 tbsp. grated fresh ginger

3-5 mint leaves

Directions:

1. Boil water in a pot.
2. Take hibiscus and ginger and blend in another pot.
3. Pour hot water over the tea mixture, cover and steep for 10-12 minutes.
4. The color of the tea will turn ruby red, then add mint leaves for fresh flavor.
5. Serve hot or cold.

Nutrition facts per serving:
Calories: 1
Carbs: 1 g

Fat: 0 g
Protein: 0 g
Sodium: 1 mg
Sugar: 0 g

Mint Tea

Fresh mint leaves give a fragrant menthol aroma, which may increase feelings of relaxation. You can use dried mint, but fresh mint has a stronger effect. Feel free to get creative and blend your favorite flavors into this tea. Both hot and cold mint teas taste very refreshing.

Serving size: make 2 servings
Brewing time: 8 minutes

Ingredients:

2 c. water

15-20 fresh mint leaves

2 lemon slices

1 tsp. honey (optional)

Directions:

1. In a teapot, boil the water.

2. Remove from the heat and add in all the mint leaves. Cover the pot and steep for 5 minutes. Increase the time for a strong flavor of mint.

3. Pour in a cup or glass.

4. Add honey and garnish with a lemon slice.

5. Enjoy hot or iced.

Nutrition facts per serving:
Calories: 150
Carbs: 26 g
Fat: 5 g
Protein: 3 g
Sodium: 75 mg
Sugar: 15 g

Sweet and Spicy Herb Tea

This tea is delicious and has a sweet and spicy taste. Make the blend and store it in an airtight tin to use as you desire.

Serving size: makes 1 serving
Brewing time: 10 minutes

Ingredients:

1 c. water

½ tbsp. cloves

1 tbsp. dried stevia

¼ c. cinnamon stick

¼ c. dried orange zest

¼ c. dried chamomile flowers

½ c. dried lemon verbena

Directions:

1. Make the blend and use 1 tsp. tea mixture.

2. Boil the water and pour it over tea mixture.

3. Cover the pot and let it steep for 5 minutes or more.

4. Strain into a cup and serve hot. Alternatively, pour over ice in the glass and serve cold.

5. Enjoy the sweet and spicy taste.

Nutrition facts per serving:

Calories: 110
Carbs: 31 g
Fat: 3 g
Protein: 2 g
Sodium: 16 mg
Sugar: 1 g

Basil Tea

Holy basil, also called Tulsi, has been used for ages for reducing fevers, relieving colds and the flu. It can also help with congestion and coughs. This is one of the most effective antiviral and antiseptic herbs. This recipe can be used for some relief from a viral infection.

Serving size: makes 1 serving
Brewing time: 5 minutes

Ingredients:

1 c. water

1 tsp. basil leaves

¼ tsp. dried ginger

½ tsp. cinnamon powder

1 tsp honey (optional)

Directions:

1. Boil the water and add the basil leaves, ginger and cinnamon.

2. Steep it for 5 minutes.

3. Strain and add honey to improve taste.

4. Pour in cup and serve hot.

Nutrition facts per serving:
Calories: 10
Carbs: 3 g

Fat: 0 g
Protein: 0 g
Sodium: 1 mg
Sugar: 0 g

Taking Care of Tea

This guide offers you a few strategies to help you preserve the freshness and quality of your tea.

The most important thing is to protect your tea from light, air, heat, odor and moisture. Exposure to air, light, and heat, can cause your tea to lose some of its flavor. Moisture is the most damaging to tea (when applied at the wrong time, of course). Teas should be stored in an airtight container made of tin or aluminum and should be kept in a dry and cool place. The refrigerator and/or freezer are not ideal places to store tea because exposure to the cold air can cause damage to the tea.

The refrigerator also contains a number of items with different odors. Tealeaves are absorbent, which means they will pull odors from their surroundings and bind with them. This can be helpful if you want to neutralize an odor, but you do not want undesirable odors in your tea either! Keep tea away from odorous things such as strong smelling foods, spices, and coffee.

Glass containers are not recommended to store tea. As mentioned, an ideal place is dark and cool. In a glass container, light can easily enter and reduce the quality of tea. As a rule, always keep your tea in a place protected from light.

Green and white teas should be consumed within three months of the date of purchase - ideally. Black tea, on the other hand, can hold its quality for approximately one year and oolong tea, about six months.

So, take care of your teas. Keep them in a dark, cool, and dry place, packed in airtight containers, away from odorous things and you will find that your tea remains fresher for a longer period of time while maintaining a great, pure taste.

A Guide to Growing Your Own Indoor Tea Garden

Would you like to take the enjoyment of tea even further? There's nothing like growing your own food! The hard work and patience that is required to grow your own food often increases one's appreciation and enjoyment of it. I may be biased, but I feel that whatever I grow myself, somehow tastes better! Like many common foods, tea can also be grown right at home.

The tea shrub *Camellia sinensis* grows up to forty feet tall; but, it is typically pruned to reach the height of about two feet. To start your garden, you will need a potting container, potting soil with natural nutrients or tea compost and your plants. If you are living in warm climate, you can grow the plant in your garden. In a cold climate, you can even grow the tea inside your house.

To begin, plant your seeds into the soil, moisten with water and leave them in the sunlight until they sprout. Once they have sprouted, you can move the plants to a place of your choice as long as it gets 6 hours of sunlight each day. Then, you water the plant regularly and let it grow for *three* years. That's right! Tea plants take upto three years before you can harvest leaves from them.

However, you don't have to start with the seeds. You can buy a plant that's already one or two-years old. Tea plants are available for sale in many local nurseries. You can do a quick search on the internet to find a location close to you where you can purchase a tea plant. The price can be anywhere from $15 to $100 depending on the kind, quality, and age of the plant. You will learn to appreciate a cup of tea like never before.

Once 3 years have passed and your plant is ready to be harvested, it is time to take your clippings to make tea. Cut the leaves off and you can prepare the tea with fresh leaves or dried leaves. Fresh leaves need to be squeezed in order to release some of their oils. Then, they will need to be placed in some kind of strainer or mesh bag. You can steep your tea in warm to hot water for about five minutes. If you would like to dry the leaves you can air-dry them, oven-dry them or use a dehydrator. Once dried, the leaves can be stored in an air tight container for months.

Besides the tea, you can mix herbs into your potting container that you can blend with your tea as well. Herbs often used with tea are lavender, chamomile, coriander, lemon balm, jasmine, mint and ginger; these are also fairly easily available at the local nursery or garden store. A small pot filled with herbs and tea is a great gift to a fellow tea lover. A gift they will enjoy for years to come.

Drinking a sip of tea from your own garden is a wonderful experience that you will surely appreciate. It is interesting to see and to be actively involved in the whole process of tea preparation.

Conclusion

We have attempted to show you throughout this book that when you drink tea, you are doing more for your body than just relaxing your mind or enjoying a beverage. By drinking tea you are actually healing your body and improving your overall health. You are also participating in a centuries old custom steeped in joy and love.

People throughout history and around the world have taken advantage of the rejuvenating effects tea has on the mind and body. This amazing beverage has spread to people of all ethnicities and ages in all corners of the world. Equipped with this knowledge about tea, accompanying herbs and their functions in the human body, you can make a truly meaningful and special cup. Whether you end up experimenting with an indoor tea garden, or purchasing your leaves elsewhere, you can make customized blends to match the needs of your mind, body, and spirit.

We hope you have enjoyed this book and found it helpful in understanding and preparing tea on a deeper level. Tea is among nature's purest of gifts to mankind and a symbol of simplicity, unity, gratitude, and love.

Enjoy!

Jenna

Made in the USA
Lexington, KY
01 April 2018